Days Out Around Fort Myers

Gillian Birch

Dedicated to the volunteers who donate their time
and talents to non-profit organizations everywhere

CONTENTS

Welcome to The Beaches of Fort Myers and Sanibel

Located on the banks of the Caloosahatchee River, Fort Myers is the historic seat of Lee County, an area known for its white sand beaches, barrier islands, golf courses, diverse fishing, shell collecting, subtropical gardens, historic attractions and year-round sunshine. No wonder it was included by Trip Advisor on its Top 10 List of Travelers' Choice® Destinations on the Rise 2012, and it continues to be one of Florida's top tourist destinations.

Developing around the three Cs of cattle, citrus and cane, downtown Fort Myers was built in the early 1900s. Much of the architecture is in fine Beaux-Arts, Neo-Classical and Art Deco style, thanks to two local business rivals who tried to outdo each other in a well-documented struggle for power in the developing city. The restored architecture, public artworks, haunted happenings and entertaining history of the founding families of Fort Myers can be enjoyed by visitors and residents alike on historian-led *True Tours* of the city. Many of the properties in downtown Fort Myers are National Historic Landmarks, yet they continue to operate as independent businesses, shops, bars and restaurants.

Early visitors to Fort Myers included inventor Thomas Edison, who was attracted by the mild winters and natural beauty of the area. The subtropical climate proved perfect for growing a banyan tree (presented to Edison by Harvey Firestone), goldenrod and other exotic plants in Edison's quest to produce cheap commercial rubber. His longtime friend and neighbor, Henry Ford, also wintered in the Fort Myers area along with the Firestones and the Burroughs families.

Nowhere captures the essence of early 20th century life for these well-heeled families better than the beautiful *Burroughs Home and Gardens* which is open daily for guided tours. The better known *Edison and Ford Winter Estates* includes a museum, botanical gardens and two historic homes, all best toured in the company of a knowledgeable guide. The newly restored research laboratory appears as it would have in Edison's time, along with a collection of early Ford motor cars. These wealthy families left a wonderful legacy that visitors to the Fort Myers area can still enjoy today. In fact, it was Thomas and Mina Edison who gifted the first avenue of royal palms along McGregor Boulevard, a tradition that has been maintained by the city ever since, leading to Fort Myers being nicknamed "City of Palms".

The city of Fort Myers takes its name from the historic fort that was built to protect 19th century settlers from the native Seminole Indians. It saw some action during the Civil War but was later abandoned. However, you can find a model of the fort and many more fascinating exhibits, displays and old photographs at the excellent *Southwest Florida Museum of History* in the old railroad depot.

Early visitors to Lee County included followers of Dr. Cyrus Teed, who established a religious community at Estero in 1893. The tranquil *Koreshan State Historic Site* has many original turn-of-the-century buildings and exotic trees gracing the banks of the Estero River.

The beaches of Fort Myers and Sanibel boast a beautiful coastline with barrier islands and inland waterways that are a joy for boating and fishing. Fort Myers Beach has miles of firm sand that is perfect for building sandcastles, and that's official. The beach hosts the American Sand Sculpting Championships each year, along with other annual events. The shallow Gulf waters are ideal for swimming, parasailing, jet skiing or for just walking along the water's edge, and the barrier islands of Sanibel and Captiva have their own appeal. Sanibel is frequently listed as one of the Top 10 Beaches in the USA. Shells wash up ankle-deep along the shoreline, but to see some really spectacular specimens you should visit the *Bailey-Matthews Shell Museum* for a truly breathtaking display.

Nearly two-thirds of Sanibel Island is a designated wildlife habitat, including the *J.N. "Ding" Darling National Wildlife Refuge*. Visitors can explore the mangroves and waterways along Wildlife Drive by tram, car, bicycle, kayak or on foot. Other places to discover Florida's unique wildlife include the *Six Mile Cypress Slough Preserve* with its 1.2 mile boardwalk and viewing platforms; the excellent *Audubon Corkscrew Swamp Sanctuary* and the family-friendly *Calusa Nature Center and Planetarium*. Alligators, otters, turtles, bobcats, wild boar, pelicans, ospreys, egrets and herons are just some of the local inhabitants that you will see on typical days out around Fort Myers.

Lakes Regional Park is the ideal place to cool off on a hot summer's day with two free splash parks, boats and kayaks for hire, and 2½ miles of winding paths which can be explored on foot or bicycle. Another popular attraction for families is the *Imaginarium* which mixes scientific hands-on activities with educational wildlife exhibits. You will find you're never too old to stroke a stingray, don special glasses in the 3D theater, try out the Hurricane Experience or apply your mind to over 60 mind-boggling challenges! From dolphin watching and sport fishing to shelling and wildlife spotting, Lee County is packed with affordable activities for all ages.

We hope you enjoy your visit to the beaches of Fort Myers and Sanibel, but be warned. Like many of the 2½ million visitors who flock to this beautiful corner of Florida every year, you might just decide you never want to leave!

NANCY HAMILTON, APR

Communications Director

THE BEACHES OF
FORT MYERS
AND SANIBEL
FORTMYERS-SANIBEL.COM

Lee County Visitor & Convention Bureau
2201 Second Street, Suite 600
Fort Myers, Florida 33901-3086

Tel: (239) 338-3500   (800) 237-6444

What's Old is New Again!

The Fort Myers River District is hopping! Come down any day of the week and you'll find plenty of things to do and see. There are unique shops, boutiques and art galleries where you can browse to your heart's content. Dine alfresco at a café or inside at one of the many award-winning restaurants. Walk along the majestic Caloosahatchee River and admire the statues in Centennial Park. But if you think the sidewalks all roll up at night, you'd be mistaken! Listen to the live music as it spills onto the street from a bar or concert. Have a nightcap while you watch a glorious sunset from a rooftop bar.

Walking around the downtown River District it's not hard to see what makes Fort Myers special. This small city has the largest concentration of historic structures south of Tampa. Not only are the buildings charming, but the stories behind them are also fascinating. Join a TrueTours walking tour and learn about how the first courthouse had no courtroom, where the Philadelphia As stayed when they came to play baseball, and how local feuds fueled the building boom of the 1920s.

The historic downtown also hosts a variety of annual events. You can watch high stepping dancers at the Celtic Festival, enjoy the illuminating parade for the Edison Festival of Light, and admire the artwork at Artsfest. There are also jazz and other music festivals and the Southwest Florida Reading Festival where you can meet some of your favorite famous authors.

Do you love the arts and museums? Check out the Sidney and Berne Davis Art Center for a performance, art exhibit or concert. See an award-winning Florida Rep play at the historic Arcade Theater. You might even be seated where Thomas Edison sat when he came to the movies. And speaking of the famous inventor, take a walk or quick drive down McGregor Boulevard and you can tour his beautiful home and grounds.

Feeling the urge to stretch on a sandy beach? Sanibel, Captiva and Fort Myers Beach are only a short ride away as are JetBlue Park and Hammond Stadium where you can catch a spring training game with the Red Sox or the Minnesota Twins.

Fort Myers has it all: shopping, restaurants, art galleries, historic walking tours, theaters, museums—and plenty of street parking and a spacious parking garage. There is something for everyone in the Fort Myers River District!

GINA TAYLOR

Gina Taylor is the former Executive Director of the Lee Trust for Historic Preservation, the first Director of the historic Burroughs Home and the former Director of the Southwest Florida Museum of History. She is the founder/owner of True Tours, Inc. and details of her five walking tours in downtown Fort Myers can be found on her website www.TrueTours.net or by calling (239) 945-0405.

Days Out Around Fort Myers

Burroughs Home and Gardens

Set in lush subtropical gardens on the banks of the Caloosahatchee River, the Burroughs Home epitomizes life for one elite family on Millionaire's Row in the early 20th century. This beautifully restored home reveals the life enjoyed by Nelson and Adeline Burroughs and their two daughters, Jettie and Mona, when Fort Myers was in its heyday.

The antique furnishings, artifacts, photographs and personal belongings of the family tell their own story within this Georgian Colonial Revival mansion. Climb the steps and enter through the grand front door with its stained glass panels. From here, knowledgeable docents will escort you back in time through the history of this local landmark which is listed on the National Register of Historic Places.

Location
Located in historic Downtown Fort Myers on the corner of Fowler and First.

2505 First Street
Fort Myers
FL33901
Tel: (239) 337-0706

http://www.burroughshome.com/

GPS Coordinates: 26.646782,-81.865738

Directions
From the north, take US-41 (S. Cleveland Ave) into Downtown Fort Myers. Once you cross over the Caloosahatchee River, take the first off-ramp into Downtown. The ramp exits onto West First Street which becomes First Street.

Turn right onto Fowler Street (one way street). Make an immediate left into the parking lot behind the red brick Langford-Kingston home (unsignposted).

Park and walk across First Street to reach the Burroughs Home.

What to Expect at Burroughs Home and Gardens

Tour groups gather in the spacious pine floored hall with its sweeping staircase. Unlike many other historic homes tours, Burroughs Home docents immediately make visitors feel at ease. They encourage you to walk around, take photographs and even take a seat in the Receiving Parlor where the tour begins.

Set in almost 2½ acres of gardens, this beautifully proportioned residence has four main receiving rooms on the first floor and four bedrooms, a study, trunk room and two bathrooms on the second floor. There is a third floor with servants' quarters which is not included in the tour. It is all topped by a Widows Walk which has splendid views across the wide Caloosahatchee River. The riverfront gardens are in the shadow of the Edison Bridge, which carries the busy southbound Business US41.

It soon becomes apparent that the 6000 square-foot Burroughs home is a cut above most estate homes. The fine woodwork, original oak and tile corner fireplaces, elegant chandeliers and burly pine wainscoting made this a very comfortable home in its time. Beautifully restored following damage from Hurricane Charlie in 2004, the house still has sliding wooden shutters on the first floor windows. They were cleverly designed to allow air to circulate while privacy was carefully maintained.

Built originally for John T. Murphy, a cattleman from Montana, the lovely Burroughs Home was actually commissioned from a catalogue. Murphy personalized the standard home with the addition of stained glass windows and other architectural embellishments. Shipped in 137 crates on four box cars, the house was delivered by railway to Punta Gorda and finished the journey by boat. Completed in 1901, the home was ahead of its time, having two full baths with indoor plumbing, electric bells to summon the servants, and it was wired throughout for electricity.

In 1918, businessman and entrepreneur Nelson Burroughs bought the home as a winter residence for his family which included his wife, Adeline, and their two daughters, Jettie and Mona. They quickly settled into the social circle in Fort Myers which included the Edisons, Fords and the Firestones. The Burroughs family hosted spectacular parties in the tropical gardens.

The tour progresses from the front parlor into the Library where Mr. Burroughs would conduct business behind the sturdy pocket doors. We admired the original chandelier fixture, family furniture and an interesting collection of old photographs before moving into the grand hall. A five-pipe annunciator is fixed to the wall and was struck to announce that dinner was served.

Near the bottom of the curved wood staircase is an unusual built-in bench seat, and a plinth where gentlemen callers for Jettie and Mona would leave their calling cards. One amusing story of the lively younger sister, Mona, was that she had a view of the bench seat lined up in her cheval mirror and would only come down to meet the visitor if she liked the look of him! Another story was that the electricity in Fort Myers was turned off nightly at 11 p.m. when everyone would retire to bed. Mona would climb down the trellis from her bedroom and cycle to the pier for late night trysts with her many admirers!

A beautiful Italian mirror tops the marble hall table beneath which is another mirror – this time for checking the petticoat and hemline before the ladies left the house. An open doorway leads to the light and airy music room on the first floor which has an Early Square Piano, an original Victrola gramophone and a fine collection of colorful pictures featuring English kings and queens.

The formal dining room has an outstanding restored mural painted on the walls depicting a typical Florida scene. Another original chandelier hangs above the dining table, which is supported on heavy carved legs with lions' heads at the top and massive claw feet. Elegant candlesticks are displayed on the buffet tables along with a selection of unusual silverware. Beyond the dining room is a well fitted Butler's Pantry with display cabinets of glassware. Behind the servants' staircase is the 1920s era kitchen with craftsman-built wall cupboards and a refrigerator with a compressor on top.

The tour continues upstairs on the generous landing and in the furnished bedrooms. Highlights include the built-in closets (an unnecessary extravagance at a time when taxes were paid on the square footage), a beautiful secretary cabinet, the trunk room and a collection of personal items belonging to Jettie and Mona. An elegant Palladian window in the study gives access to the front balcony.

A set of photographs and an interesting letter from Edison to Ford about his thoughts on the dangers of smoking (blaming the cigarette paper rather than the tobacco!) make fascinating exhibits. There is also a Charles Lindberg display commemorating the first trans-Atlantic flight from New York to Paris in 1927.

Outdoors is a covered oval terrace and steps lead down into the gardens where live oaks covered in resurrection ferns and Spanish moss shade much of the property. A fountain, gazebo, and an early grotto fed by an artesian well are pointed out as we stroll along the paths.

The caretaker's house and carriage house, which once housed a pair of Rolls Royce Phantoms belonging to the Burroughs sisters, takes up much of the grounds.

Hidden in the ficus and bougainvillea is the entrance to the "secret" garden. High tea is still served in the garden on occasion, next to the reflecting pool.

Burroughs Home and Gardens was deeded to the City of Fort Myers by Mona Burroughs Fischer when she died in 1978. Her wish was that it should be used as a park, library or museum and she would surely have approved of its continued public use today.

Additional Info

Now owned by the City of Fort Myers, the Burroughs Home is managed by the Uncommon Friends Foundation. It makes the perfect venue for social events, weddings and charity fundraisers.

Admission

Adults $12; Seniors $10
Children 6-12 $5; aged 5 and under free

Guided Tour Times

Monday through Friday at 11 a.m. and 1 p.m.
Group tours can be arranged by special request.

Where to Eat near the Burroughs Home

A short stroll along First Street will bring you to a choice of excellent places to eat. The French Connection on the corner of First and Jackson serves excellent light lunches, salads and crepes.

It's hard to miss the Ford's Garage restaurant in the Dean building further along First Street. This service-station-themed eatery has an Old Ford Model T parked outside, oil rags in hose clips are novelty napkins and all the signature burgers are named after local celebrities!

Finally, and most in keeping with the Burroughs home atmosphere, enjoy dining in style at the award-winning Verandah Restaurant. The Zagat-rated menu and turn-of-the-century architecture are sure to make your historic experience in Downtown Fort Myers complete.

Nearby Attractions

- TrueTours Historical Walking Tours
- South West Florida Museum of History
- Imaginarium Science Center
- Calusa Nature Center and Planetarium

TrueTours Historical Walking Tours

Ably led by local resident and historian Gina Taylor, the Downtown Historical Walking Tour is one of five themed tours which give visitors an insight into the fascinating history and architecture of Fort Myers.

The Historic Downtown Fort Myers River District has an extraordinary story to tell. The downtown area of this lovely city is listed on the National Register of Historic Places as a Commercial District, and First Street in particular has some exceptionally beautiful architecture spanning the last century.

The Historical Walking Tour tells the fascinating story behind these lovely restored buildings which are mainly attributable to two local businessmen who became bitter rivals. Buildings particularly worth looking out for include the Dean building, the Arcade Theatre, the city's first eight-floor skyscraper, the historic Earnhardt building, the Sidney and Berne Davis Arts Center building and the Beaux-Arts First National Bank of Fort Myers, the only granite building in the city.

Other noteworthy places on the tour include the award-winning marina which is the longest continuously running marina in Florida, the Richards Building which boasted the first elevator in the city, the Robb and Stucky Furniture Store with the first Coca-Cola vending machine, the restored Court House and the oak tree outside, now an eagle sculpture, termites permitting!

Location
Historic Downtown Fort Myers River District

The tour starts from the Franklin Shops, 2200 First Street

Tel: (239) 945-0405 for reservations

www.Truetours.net

GPS Coordinates: 26.6463, -81.8705

Directions

From US41, follow signs to the Historic District of Fort Myers. The tour starts from the Franklin Shops on First Street

What to Expect on a Historic Walking Tour

The 90-minute Historical Walking Tour begins right outside the Franklin Shops, built in 1937 as a hardware store and still retains the original name in the terrazzo floor at the entrance.

After a brief introduction to the location, which has the largest concentration of original buildings in South West Florida, our guide began the fascinating history of Fort Myers, describing its early days as a pioneering cattle town accessible only by boat. Originally the location of Fort Harvey, you will hear how it was renamed Fort Myers in 1850 as a rather unorthodox wedding gift in honor of Colonel Abraham Myers, son-in-law of the fort's commander, Major General David E. Twiggs.

The transformation of Fort Myers from its decline in the 1960s to the present day success began with the pavement in First Street. When the city undertook a $50 million project to bury the utilities underground, they found beneath the streets the original red brick paving which they decided to have cleaned and re-laid. This was the start of a huge restoration project of the historic buildings which line First Street, parts of Main Street, Bay Street and the Theatre Arcade.

The tour moves slowly along the street from one set of benches to the next to admire the Dean building, now housing Ford's Garage Café. The building began life as a small hotel in the 1920s but quickly expanded a whole block to accommodate the Philadelphia A's Baseball Team who were invited to train in Fort Myers.

Continue down the narrow Bay View Court to reach Bay Street, alas no longer on the waterfront, and learn about the city's four piers which were once a hive of activity. They received supplies for the fort and dispatched fruit from the local citrus packing plant, the largest in the world at that time. Of course, the Pleasure Pier was the most interesting piece of history, now long gone. However, one part of the Pleasure Palace has survived in the unlikely form of the second floor dance hall, complete with its wooden floors and domed roof. In 1943 this upper story was removed when the pier became unstable and was moved to the Riverfront where it now forlornly awaits its fate. Known as the "Hall of 50 States" it accommodated many parties hosted by the Edisons, Fords, Firestones, and other influential families who had winter homes in the city.

The walking tour continues through the Theatre Arcade, probably the city's first shopping mall, with its small shops and boutiques opening onto the central covered walkway. One building after another is highlighted and its history retold as the tour explores the busy streets. See the grand Neo-Classical keystone building, built originally as a Post Office and now housing the Sidney and Berne Davis Art Museum. You can almost picture local socialites such as the Burroughs sisters hanging out with Connie Mack and the Philly A baseball players in this lively city in the early 20th century.

The tour commentary reveals that we have two local businessmen to thank for the exceptional quality and proliferation of local buildings along First Street. After a falling out between bank owner Harvie E. Heitman and board member Mr Langford, the rivalry between these two wealthy and successful entrepreneurs exploded into a fierce competition. They both began buying up land along First Street and developing it at a furious rate.

When Mr Heitman built his Bank of Fort Myers, now housing the French Connection Café, he installed a fireplace and rocking chairs to create a user-friendly ambience. Mr Langford went one better one, creating the lovely granite building in Beaux-Arts style on the corner of First and Hendry Streets. It still has the sign of the First National Bank and the date MCMVII (1907) over the grand pillared entrance, although it now houses law offices. They both built theaters and fought over the patronage of the Edisons and the Fords.

More local stories unfold as the walking tour progresses around to Morgan House with its castellated roofline and rooftop bar. Hear how a pen of baby alligators became an enterprising sightseeing attraction to draw shoppers into the area which lacked the foot traffic of First Street. The tour pauses near the stunning turquoise and pink Art Deco Edison Theater, now used as offices. Here you will learn how Lee County came into being, although the building of a suitable Court House took a little longer than anticipated.

The tour continues through the arcade of the Indigo Hotel which has wonderful scenic views from the rooftop bar. Listen to the story behind the amazing 100 foot long tile mosaic in the courtyard. It depicts the history of Fort Myers including the sad defeat which marked the end of the Seminole Wars when the Seminole Indians were relocated to Oklahoma. Finally the tour, and the amazing story of Fort Myers, comes to an end back on First Street.

This Historic Walking Tour brings to life the enthusiasm and dedication of countless local people who fought to make Fort Myers what it was and is today. Enthusiastically told by a local guide, it certainly made me want to move to Fort Myers immediately and be part of this thriving Arts City!

Additional Info
Reservations are required by phone or email for all tours.

As well as the Historical Walking Tour, True Tours also offers the following tours on various days:

Public Art Tour – Focusing on the artists, art panels and sculptures in Downtown Fort Myers (90 minutes)

Architecture Tour – Highlighting the architecture in Downtown Fort Myers, including examples of Neo Classical, Beaux-Arts and Art Deco structures (75 minutes)

Downtown Revitalization Tour – Appreciate the transformation of the historic Downtown District from its decline in the 1960s to its present day award-winning redevelopment (60 minutes)

Haunted History Tour – Delve into local history and hear sinister stories of residential and commercial properties reputed to have paranormal activity (90 minutes)

Sunday Brunch and Historical Walking Tour – Historical Walking Tour plus Sunday brunch at the Broadway Bistro and admission to the Edison Ford Winter Estates – a full day!

Cost

TrueTours Historic Walking Tour
Adults $10; Students $6
Other tours vary in price

Historical Tour Times
Wednesday through Sunday at 10.30 a.m. daily

1st Friday of the month there is an additional walking tour at 5 p.m. before the monthly Art Walk

Where to Eat in Downtown Fort Myers

Fort Myers is packed with great places to eat at very competitive prices. The Zagat-rated Verandah Restaurant on Second Street is one of the best, and in a historic building too. Ford's Garage Café on First Street offers Burgers of Fame with Black Angus burgers named after local dignitaries and napkins that look like oil rags! I never thought I would see chips and gravy on the menu outside the UK, but they do them here.

The interior of the Firestone Grille on Bay Street features tires running around the upper level décor and the SkyBar is THE place to watch the sunset. Just along First Street from the Franklin shops is the French Connection which is always a popular destination. Did I say you would be spoiled for choice?

Nearby Attractions
- Edison & Ford Winter Estates
- Burroughs Home and Gardens
- Southwest Florida Museum of History
- Imaginarium

Southwest Florida Museum of History

Established in 1982 and housed in the original railroad station buildings of the Atlantic Coast Line Railroad, the Southwest Florida Museum of History welcomes over 15,000 visitors every year. The spacious, well-laid out exhibits tell the history of this corner of Southwest Florida from the time of the dinosaurs through the 20th century. Surprisingly large, the exhibits bring the story of Fort Myers and the surrounding area vividly to life through its various commercial enterprises. Lumber, citrus, cattle ranching and the arrival of the railroad are all portrayed with displays of equipment, photographs, models and personal belongings donated by local residents.

Explore the informative exhibits, listen to local residents sharing their personal recollections of life in Fort Myers, step aboard the restored 1929 Pullman railcar and take a look inside a typical Cracker home.

The permanent displays are accompanied by an informative commentary provided on an audio wand which is available in various languages.

Location
Located 4 miles west of I-75 exit 138, the museum is one block south of Dr. Martin Luther King Jr Blvd

2031 Jackson St
Fort Myers
FL33901
Tel: (239) 321-7430

www.museumofhistory.org/

GPS Coordinates: 26.639994,-81.866504

Directions
From I-75 take exit 138 and follow signs to downtown Fort Myers.

Take Hwy 82 east from Fort Myers city center and shortly turn right onto Jackson Street. The museum and car park are on the left side of the street.

What to Expect at the Southwest Florida Museum of History

Step through the doors of the former Railroad building and turn back time as you explore the various sets and exhibits depicting life in this colorful former cattle town. Arranged in chronological order, the first displays are of the skull and fossilized teeth of a Megalodon, the largest shark on earth that lived in the seas covering Florida during the age of the dinosaurs.

The local history lesson continues with displays of shells and artifacts left behind by the Calusa people, known as the "Shell Indians" who lived on the sandy shores around Fort Myers and Sanibel Island. They lived on fish and seafood and used shells for tools, utensils and jewelry. Their discarded shell mounds have been excavated to provide a rich source of information about the history of the area. Native Indian history continues with more up-to-date accounts of the battles between the Seminoles and the Army before Billy Bowlegs and his followers were relocated to Indian Territory in Oklahoma.

Exhibits of the 1865 Battle of Fort Myers, the southernmost land battle of the American Civil War, includes a model of the battlefield and the layout of the original fort, circa 1850, which gave the city its name.

The local lumber trade is represented with a model of a saw mill followed by exhibits of the three Cs of Florida agriculture – cattle, citrus and cane. Florida's colorful Cracker history is all about the Florida cowboys. Museum exhibits, photographs and informative storyboards recapture the late 19th century era when Fort Myers was a major area for cattle ranching. Rancher Jacob Summerlin, whose name is immortalized in various Fort Myers landmarks, apparently had a thriving business driving cattle across Florida to the busy river port of Fort Myers.

Further on in the museum is an interesting account of Florida's early Citrus Trade. The 1894 "Big Squeeze Freeze" saw temperatures drop as low as 24°F which killed most citrus plantations further north. Many citrus farmers relocated to Fort Myers and the area saw a 260% increase in citrus exports shipped out from the local piers on the Caloosahatchee River. Old photographs, packing boxes and primitive machinery capture the era, along with relics from the sugar cane industry, which in 1887 was second only to cattle export in the Fort Myers area.

More up-to-date exhibits include the arrival of one of Fort Myers' most famous residents, Thomas Edison and his wife Mina. They left a wonderful legacy with their historic estate and the royal palms they planted along McGregor Blvd, earning Fort Myers the title "City of Palms".

The arrival of the railway in 1904 saw many more visitors arriving in Fort Myers for business and pleasure. The original wooden depot on Monroe Street was replaced by the Atlantic Coast Train Depot in 1924. The building was well used until 1971 when the passenger service finally ended. A porter's barrow and an old shoeshine stand recapture those not-so-distant days.

In 1982 the dilapidated depot reopened as the new home of the Southwest Florida Museum of History. Wandering around the exhibits you can still see the segregated waiting areas for passengers, separating black passengers from whites with a fine brass rail. The two sets of ticket windows remain, although the original open arches leading out from the verandah are now bricked up. One of the original waiting rooms, complete with original fireplace and tile flooring, is now used for showing a 30-minute film of local life through the eyes of various residents entitled *Untold Stories of Fort Myers*.

A beautifully crafted model of First Street in turn-of-the-century Fort Myers captures the attention of most museum visitors. It shows a row of businesses that existed on First Street in 1900 and was recreated by Mini-DeLites Club from photographs and archives to ensure accuracy. The recreated miniature interiors show Blount's General Store, Fort Myers Press, the Women's Club Reading Room, the local drug store owned by E.M. Williams, Foxworthy's clothing store, the Silver King Saloon, Heitman Grocery, the Lightsey Butcher Shop and Ike Shaw Taxidermy. You can also peek inside the offices of Hendry Attorney, Battery and Owens Insurance and the Lee County Telephone Exchange.

Fire service and military history uniforms and memorabilia add to the collection of indoor artifacts which include a 1926 La France Pumper. Other relics from early 20th century Fort Myers include the early telephone switchboard and a buggy used by Dr. M. F. Johnson who served the community until well into his 80s. Life on the Caloosahatchee River is depicted by the old wooden boat *Aunt Jemima* which was used to haul boats in and out of storage at Hanson's boatyard.

The museum tour continues outside with the 83-foot railcar which is hard to miss. Although rather uninspiring on the outside, the interior of the Esperanza railcar has been restored to its 1920s state of luxury. It is fascinating to be able to climb aboard and walk through the exhibit admiring the leather seats, staff call buttons, personalized china, brass fixtures and Cuban mahogany fitments. Primitive air conditioning was provided by a block of ice carried at the front of the car which cooled the incoming air before it circulated through vents to each carriage!

Informative signboards showed that the railcar cost $80,000 to build and a similar amount to run each year, so it was a pretty exclusive way to travel. It includes three state rooms with fold-down bunks and clever commode/sink combination units. A lounge, private dining car for eight, galley kitchen and servants' quarters show how life was enjoyed by the wealthier families in the early 1930s and this was certainly one of the highlights of my visit.

After that, head over to view the simpler furnishings of the recreated Cracker home nearby. These were the typical residences of local cattlemen and their families, built of cedar and yellow pine with a high airy ceiling, sloping tin roof and a shady front porch. Just beyond the huge mahogany tree is the Combat Infantrymen's Memorial in the grounds of the museum.

At the end of the tour, return your audio wand to the museum gift shop and browse some of the interesting local books, replica historic scrolls and other unusual toys and gifts on sale. The helpful staff are extremely knowledgeable about the museum and the depot building and are happy to answer questions.

Admission
Adults $9.50
Seniors $8.50
Students $5

Admission includes the self-guided audio tour

Opening Times
Tuesdays through Saturdays 10 a.m. to 5 p.m.

Where to Eat near the Southwest Florida Museum of History
The Twisted Vine Bistro on Bay Street is an informal place to dine at lunchtime. It has a pleasant outdoor courtyard with a great atmosphere for enjoying drinks and appetizers. Alternatively, First Street has a good choice of cafés, coffee shops and restaurants.

For lighter fare, the acclaimed Wisteria Tea Room on Second Street is open from 11-3pm daily and does excellent afternoon tea.

Main dining section of the Esperanza railcar

Nearby Attractions

- TrueTours Historical Walking Tours
- Edison and Ford Winter Estates
- Imaginarium
- Calusa Nature Center and Planetarium

Imaginarium Science Center

The hands-on Imaginarium Science Center and Aquarium at Fort Myers is an experience beyond your wildest imagination! Kids will love the fun activities both indoors and outside, and adults will not be able to resist having a go themselves and becoming equally absorbed in the different challenges, experiments and logic puzzles.

The admission cost includes entry to the 3D film theater (special glasses are provided), Science Shows, Live Animal Encounters, Touch Tanks, Stingray Feeding, IMAG-TV, Hurricane Experience, Caloosahatchee Experience and over 60 hands-on science exhibits.

Allow a full day to enjoy this amazing family attraction which will be the highlight of any weekend trip or vacation.

Location
On the corner of Dr Martin Luther King Jr Blvd (Hwy 82) and Cranford Ave in Fort Myers.

2000 Cranford Avenue
Fort Myers
FL33916
Tel: (239) 321-7420

www.imaginariumfortmyers.com/

GPS Co-ordinates: 26.640144,-81.859329

Directions
From Hwy 41 (Tamiami Trail), head east on Dr Martin Luther King Jr Blvd (Hwy 82) for ½ mile before turning right into Cranford Ave.

The Imaginarium car park is immediately on the right beneath the colorful water tower.

What to Expect at the Imaginarium

The Imaginarium is a huge two-story fun palace crammed with fun games, logic puzzles, experiences and video games. The fun continues outdoors in the surrounding grounds with the Caloosahatchee Experience. The exhibits aim to make learning about science and natural history fun for all ages. Learning through discovery and play makes this a fantastic day out for youngsters and gives families of all ages a chance to bond and learn together.

Check out the times of the special daily activities to make sure you don't miss out on any of the fun experiences. Animal encounters, stingray feeding, supervised touch-tank experiences, the Hurricane Experience and 3D films are the highlights of any visit and they are scheduled to take place at set times during the day, so check your program.

The first animal encounter you will see is the Stingray Pool where velvety stingrays can be fed from the palm of your hand (additional $3 per ticket) and stroked for an amazing close encounter with marine life.

Further along there are a series of stations with logic puzzles laid out and an Idea Lab to challenge adults and youngsters alike. Prove Newton's Law of Motion with a ball experiment or head for the Dinosaur Exhibit and dig for prehistoric fossils. Beat the goalkeeper in the Sporty Science Area of Team Imaginarium where you try to score a goal against the virtual goalie. The cheering crowd and ref's whistle add to the atmosphere of this very realistic experience and you even get to see replays of your attempt on goal. You can also see the speed of the ball and the scoreboard of hits and misses, whether you choose to play soccer, basketball or hockey.

Learn more about momentum with the Build Your Own Roller Coaster exhibit or visit Tiny Town where there are plenty of chunky building bricks, paper, crayons and games laid out for pre-school visitors as well as a Puppet Theater for more imaginative guests. Challenging video games include following the Scout Markers to keep the dinosaur fed and watered.

In another area, the shallow Sea-to-See Touch Tanks have porcupine puffer fish, Spanish lobsters, sea stars and urchins with brightly decorated shells, displaying just some of the wonders of the underwater world.

Step inside the Storm Experience for rain, thunder and lightning or line up for the Storm Smart Hurricane Experience simulator where visitors can enter a chamber and feel the force of 45 mph winds for real. Goggles are provided for this memorable experience. Other exhibits demonstrate how impact-resistant windows and new types of flexible window shutters can protect Florida homes from hurricane damage in real life.

Make your own news program and see it live on IMAG-TV or learn about the planets in more hands-on science exhibits. Another quiet corner is the Discovery Lab where youngsters (and adults!) pore over a series of slides with the aid of a microscope. In the Animal Nano Lab, aquariums display reefs, young alligators, snakes and colorful toads.

Doors lead outside to the 3D Theater where during my visit the 20-minute 3D film entitled Dinosaurs – Giants of Patagonia took viewers back to prehistoric times when these giants roamed the earth. See how paleontologists work to uncover the fossilized remains and learn how these animals hunted for food. Films are changed regularly to keep the interest for repeat visitors.

Further along in the garden is Fish Eye Lagoon where huge Japanese koi and various duck species hang around the boardwalk hoping to be fed. More reptiles and turtles can be found around the garden along with a recreated model of the Caloosa Locks and Dam. Visitors can turn the wheel to open and close the lock gates and see how they work.

I was really impressed by the enormous variety and quality of exhibits the Imaginarium packs in. It is a really wonderful place to bring children of all ages. They will certainly never be bored for a moment and the huge number of different activities makes this attraction excellent value for money.

The Imaginarium Shop is worth a browse before you leave as it has a good selection of scientific toys at pocket-money prices – great to put away for a rainy day!

Additional Info
Friday Family Nights run from 5 p.m. to 8 p.m. with family admission packages and dinner packages available.
Other programs include Spring Break Sessions, Summer Camp, Homeschool Days and Preschool Programs.

Admission

Adults (13+)	$12
Seniors (55+)	$10
Students (3-17)	$8

Children 2 and under FREE

Hand feeding stingrays (limited number of tickets) $3

Opening Times

Tuesday to Saturday 10 a.m. to 5 p.m.

Late night Fridays until 8 p.m; Sundays Noon to 5 p.m.

Closed Mondays

Where to Eat at the Imaginarium

Rockin' Rays Stingray Café means you don't have to tear youngsters away from the fun at lunchtime. Snacks, hot dogs, burgers, pizza, nachos, sodas and ice cream are all served here from 11.30 a.m. to 2 p.m. Meals are sensibly priced from $4.

Nearby Attractions

- Southwest Florida Museum of History
- Burroughs Home and Gardens
- TrueTours Historical Walking Tours

Edison and Ford Winter Estates′

Located on 20 acres of prime riverfront in Fort Myers are the historic winter homes of two of America's most historic figures – Thomas Edison and Henry Ford. Now wonderfully restored and managed by a non-profit corporation, these landmark homes are one of the main attractions in the area.

The site includes Seminole Lodge, Edison's Winter Home built in 1885, along with an adjacent guest house. Next door is The Mangoes which Ford purchased in 1916. There is also a caretaker's cottage, a swimming pool, the original Botanic Research Laboratory and a number of other buildings set in the extensive gardens spanning either side of the busy palm-lined McGregor Boulevard.

With an extensive banyan tree covering one acre of gardens, a garage with early Ford vehicles, a Visitor Center, Museum, outdoor Banyan Café and a well-stocked Garden Shop, the attraction offers a full day of educational tours and things to see and do.

Location
Just south of downtown Fort Myers on the banks of the Caloosahatchee River.

2350 McGregor Blvd
Fort Myers
FL33901
Tel: (239) 334-7419

www.edisonfordwinterestates.org

GPS Coordinates: 26.634754,-81.879971

Directions
From I-75 take exit 136 and follow Hwy 884 (Colonial Blvd) West.
After crossing Hwy 41 keep in the right lane. Turn right into McGregor Blvd.
After approximately 2 miles the entrance to the Edison Ford Estate car park is on the right

Things to Do at the Edison Ford Winter Estates
After parking beneath the shady trees, start your visit at the Ticket Office where you can book a place on various tours or take a self-guided tour of the estate. One of the most

informative and comprehensive tours is the historian-led Behind the Scenes Tour which takes place at specific times each week. It takes two hours to cover all the properties and the newly restored Laboratory. There are various shorter tours available and a self-guided audio tour of the houses for those wanting to explore the attraction at their own pace.

Most tours begin in the auditorium in the far corner of the Estates Museum. If you have time before your tour, browse around the eclectic collection of museum exhibits which include many of Edison's inventions along with family memorabilia and old photographs.

Edison is best known for inventing the phonograph which was later adapted to record and play music. This was remarkable as he was actually almost completely deaf. He was a prolific inventor and altogether he had over 1000 patents for his inventions including a motion picture camera and his long-lasting electric light bulb.

First stop on the tour is the Botanical Laboratory which resembles in some ways Edison's Menlo Park lab. He spent several months each winter in Florida but it was never his main home. Built in 1928, the laboratory resembles a machine shop with a chemical processing area, distillation apparatus, a plant grinding room, office and a dark room. A single five-horsepower engine drove a shaft with a variety of belts connecting the various machines. Restored in 2012 at a cost of $1 million, work benches are still laid out with bottles and test tubes, just as if Edison had stepped out for a moment.

One of Edison's main projects in Florida was to find a reliable source of latex for making rubber, hence his planting of various fig species including the banyan, which is now the largest in the USA.

After stopping to photograph the banyan tree with its many aerial roots, cross the road to the main gardens and historic homes. The path leads past the cracker-style house that was once the home of Edison's caretaker. The structure already existed on the land when Edison bought it and is the oldest surviving structure in Fort Myers. The garages and apartment above were added later. The building was originally used as a stopover for cattle drovers moving their herds down the dusty thoroughfare that has since become McGregor Blvd. When the Edisons moved to Fort Myers, cattle ranching was the main business in the area and there were fewer than 350 residents.

The gardens are blooming with color in early summer with hibiscus, euphorbia, trumpet trees, tulip trees, poinciana, gingers, orchids and many other gorgeous subtropical flowers. Each well-tended plant is clearly labeled, making any tour of the gardens a real treat for gardeners. The Moonlight Garden with a small reflecting pool is one of the most tranquil spots and marks the footprint of Edison's original laboratory which was eventually moved by Ford to Greenfield Village, a collection of historically significant buildings located in Dearborn, Michigan.

Take a look at the above-ground swimming pool enjoyed by the six Edison children and visit the lily pond, pier and fountain. Banana plants, mango trees, bamboo stands and an avenue of royal palms are the main botanical highlights of the gardens. Incidentally, the Edisons donated the first mile of royal palms lining McGregor Blvd. The tradition has been continued by the city and Fort Myers is now known as the "City of Palms."

Most tours only allow visitors to look through the open doors and windows into the ground floor rooms of Seminole Lodge to minimize wear and tear. However, the Behind the Scenes Tour does allow visitors access inside and upstairs and protective shoe covers are provided.

Seminole Lodge is filled with the original Edison furnishings which consist mainly of simple rattan seating, tables and bookcases. Of great interest are the individually designed brass "electroliers", which eventually replaced chandeliers and gasoliers in most American homes.

The accommodation is divided between the original family house and the guest house, which are linked by a long pergola. The guest house originally belonged to Edison's partner and friend, Ezra Gilliland. After a falling out, Edison eventually bought the house and remodeled it to provide a kitchen, dining room and extra bedrooms.

The next major building is The Mangoes, a similar structure covered in white cladding with generous porches providing shady seating areas. Built in 1911 for Robert Smith, when it came up for sale in 1916 Henry Ford bought it and spent several weeks each winter at this retreat. It has period furnishings, although unfortunately they are not the original Ford belongings.

After browsing around the homes and the Ford Automobile Exhibit where historic vehicles are on display, the final stop should be at the Ford Cottage Shoppe, once the caretaker's house on the Ford Estate.

Return across the road to browse the competitively priced nursery, gift shop, café and museum.

Additional Info

Monthly special tours and events such as the Antique Car Show are worth looking out for, as is the Holiday Nights Tour during December.

A beautiful guide book filled with color photographs of the property is available for just $3.

Best value admission is annual membership which is $55 for individuals and $75 for couples. As well as offering unlimited admission, it includes special tours, membership benefits and discounts to other historic homes.

Admission

General Admission Adults	$20 (includes orientation, audio tour and admission to the Lab and Museum)
Lab and Museum Adults	$12
Historian-led Tour Adults	$25
Behind the Scenes Adults	$40
Garden Tour Adults	$40
River Cruises Adults	$45 including admission to the estate and a cruise of the Caloosahatchee River with a stop for lunch at the Royal Palm Yacht Club

Please note that tour times may vary seasonally, so it is advisable to call ahead or check the website for availability and current prices.

Opening Times

9 a.m. to 5.30 p.m. daily, excluding Thanksgiving and Christmas Day

Where to Eat Around the Edison Ford Estates

The onsite café offers a selection of sandwiches, snacks and salads. There are also picnic tables in the gardens.

Further south on McGregor Blvd (about 1.7 miles) is the Edison Restaurant and Bar at the Fort Myers Country Club. Enjoy dining at the outdoor tables overlooking the golf course, take a booth in the library-themed area of the Porch and Terrace Bar or sample upscale dining in the elegant restaurant.

Nearby Attractions

- TrueTours Historical Walking Tours
- Burroughs Home and Gardens
- South West Florida Museum of History
- Imaginarium

Lakes Regional Park

It's not easy to occupy younger visitors without spending a fortune, but the Lakes Regional Park on Gladiolus Drive is a great find. This large park covers 279 acres and has plenty of car parking (nominal hourly rate payable at the machine), over two miles of boardwalks and trails, lakes (of course!) with wildlife, and free guided walks on Saturdays.

There are boats, bicycles and surreys to rent and a miniature railroad running around the park's features. Best of all, the park has two children's water splash areas with fountains, and several free internet hotspots.

The park was developed in 1984 from a former quarry and the lakes are natural. Like much of Florida the area is barely above the water table. Lakes cover a total of 158 acres of the 279-acre park. The water in the lakes is from rainfall and runoff and is up to 20 feet deep in places.

On Friday mornings the car park hosts a Farmer's Market with produce from the area, but this only takes place in the winter season, November through April. Close to the main parking lot there is a botanical garden with a few flowers and shrubs. If you fancy hosting a get-together or children's party, pavilions are available for private hire.

Location
Located on the corner of Hwy 41 and Gladiolus Drive

7330 Gladiolus Drive
Fort Myers
FL33908
Tel: (239) 533-7575

http://www.leeparks.org/facility-info/facility-details.cfm?Project_Num=0101

GPS Coordinates: 26.528037,-81.877151

Directions
Drive south on US41 from downtown Fort Myers for about 8 miles. Turn right into Gladiolus Drive and immediately right again into Lakes Regional Park.

What to Expect at Lakes Regional Park

The extensive lakes make this a very scenic and pleasant park for walking, cycling and jogging. There are several loop trails which altogether offer 2½ miles of winding paths through native vegetation.

The park never seems to be overcrowded despite clearly being popular with local families at weekends. Fishing is permitted and there are bass, catfish and bream in the lakes. The reeds and shallows are always frequented by ibis, egrets and herons, especially at nesting time. The overhanging tree branches are a good place to spot anhingas spreading their black wings to dry after a dive for fish and frogs.

Children will enjoy spotting the turtles that come from far and wide if you feed the ducks some bread! There are signs warning about alligators, but I have never actually seen any sign of one. However, swimming is not permitted in the lakes.

Youngsters love to ride the red Miniature Railroad Train which takes riders around the park, passing scale models of buildings and running through a short tunnel. The ride lasts 15 minutes and currently is $1 for young children and $5 for accompanying adults. Note that young children are not allowed to ride alone! There is a large playground with climbing equipment, swings, slides, a cafeteria and concessions selling drinks and ices.

41

Visitors will certainly enjoy the free waterpark areas that have water fountains, jets and other water amusements in the enclosed splash zone. It is the perfect place to head for on the hot, sticky summer days of Florida, and the area is well-used from Easter to Thanksgiving.

Guided walks are offered in the park with volunteer naturalists. On the first Saturday in the month you can join Bird Patrol Volunteers on a walking tour from 8.30 a.m. to 10.30 a.m. The walk explores the natural habitat and walkers can spot birds and wildlife in season. More details are available by calling (239) 533-7440.

On the second Saturday of the month the Master Gardener leads tours of the Botanical Garden from 9 a.m. to 10 a.m.

The third Saturday is "Children's Walk in the Garden" day, again from 9 a.m. to 10 a.m. and full details are available from the L.P. Enrichment Foundation by calling (239) 533-7575.

All these events are free, but there is a fee for parking.

Additional Info
Pets, alcohol and motorized vehicles are not allowed in Lakes Park and swimming is not permitted in the lake.

You can bring your laptop and make use of the free internet access at Parking lots 1 and 2, the beach area and pavilions A1, A2, A3, A4, B1, B2 and D1.

Admission

Lakes Regional Park has free admission but there is a fee for parking, currently $1 per hour, max. $5 per day.

Train Rides

1-5 years	$1
6 years and up	$4

Holiday train rides add $1 to the above prices

Rentals per hour including equipment
Boats

Single Kayak	$10
Double Kayak	$15
Pedal Boat	$20
Double Pedal Boat	$25

Bikes

Single Surrey	$15
Double Surrey	$25
Deuce Coupe	$15
Chopper	$10
Quad Sport	$10
Slingshot	$10
Cruiser Bike	$8
Scooter	$5

Opening Times

Lakes Park is open every day from 7 a.m. to dusk.
Water features are open from 9 a.m. to 6 p.m. but they close daily for maintenance from 12.30 p.m. to 1.30 p.m.

Where to Eat near Lakes Park

There are snacks and food available at the bike rental centers near the beach and at the Train Interpretive Center.

There are plenty of benches and picnic tables around the lake if you want to bring your own food and drink.

Nearby Attractions

- Calusa Nature Center and Planetarium
- Six Mile Cypress Slough Preserve
- Imaginarium
- Fort Myers Beach

J.N. "Ding" Darling National Wildlife Refuge

Over two-thirds of Sanibel Island is designated as a wildlife habitat, much of it within the "Ding" Darling National Wildlife Refuge. The area is manned by 260 volunteers who can be seen along the Wildlife Road and trails helping visitors to spot and identify the resident birds and wildlife.

The Refuge has an excellent Education/Visitor Center which has recreated displays of local wildlife. It hosts many events including films and a free series of lectures which take place on Fridays in the auditorium throughout the winter season. Maps, leaflets and information are available about the wildlife, birds, turtles and other inhabitants of the refuge.

There is a recreation of "Ding" Darling's studio complete with drawing board and a selection of his sketches and cartoons. There is also a well-stocked gift shop with nature-themed gifts and a good selection of books for sale.

The "Ding" Darling National Wildlife Refuge is part of the largest undeveloped mangrove ecosystem in the U.S. Known for its migratory birds in spring and fall, it is one of 550 Wildlife Refuges in the country.

This spectacular wildlife habitat was declared the Sanibel National Wildlife Refuge in 1945, thanks to the efforts of cartoonist Jay Norwood Darling, affectionately known by his pen name "Ding", an abbreviation of his last name. The refuge was later renamed in his honor in 1967. Initially the area was only accessible by boat. Wildlife Drive was created in the 1960s and took one man four years to cut and dredge the route and build the existing causeway.

The Wildlife Refuge covers 6,400 acres of mangrove forest, shallow seagrass beds, wetlands, marshes and hardwood hammocks. A single track one-way road runs for four miles through the reserve. It allows visitors to enjoy many recreational pastimes and see a variety of native Florida wildlife in its natural environment.

The refuge is home to alligators, turtles, otters, bobcats, raccoons, possums, crabs, many species of saltwater fish and over 220 species of birds.

Location
2 miles west of Tarpon Bay Road on Sanibel-Captiva Road

1 Wildlife Drive
Sanibel
FL33957
Tel: (239) 472-1100 (Visitor Center)
Tel: (239) 472-1351 (Tram tour bookings and enquiries)

www.fws.gov.dingdarling

GPS Coordinates: 26.445277,-82.11264

Directions
After crossing the toll bridge onto Sanibel Island, head west along Periwinkle Way and follow the signs for Captiva.

After joining Sanibel-Captiva Road, the "Ding" Darling Natural Wildlife Refuge is about 1½ miles on the right.

What to Expect on a Tram Tour with Tarpon Bay Explorers
There are many ways to enjoy a visit to the "Ding" Darling Natural Wildlife Refuge, but the very best way to learn more about the wildlife and the environment is on a guided tram tour which is run as a concession.

Starting from the car park, the tram tours take approximately 1¾ hours and depart hourly. Reservations are recommended but you can usually just turn up and join a tour in the quieter seasons.

Our guide for the eco-tour was Mari, an enthusiastic and lively naturalist who kept us well-informed with her knowledgeable commentary both on and off the open-sided tram.

The "Ding" Darling Refuge is one of the Top 10 in the US for birders and the refuge is enjoyed by around 800,000 visitors each year.

The drive is a four-mile rough surface road on top of a dike. It is strictly one-way for all traffic and parking is allowed on the right-hand side of the road for cars to stop and observe wildlife.

Cyclists and walkers can detour off the Wildlife Road onto separate trails such as the two-mile Indigo Trail which gives them close contact with the marshes and pools.

The road has ditches and lakes on either side and in the tangle of mangrove roots we could see small fish hiding in relative safety from their larger predators. Crabs, worms, mollusks and shrimps also make their home in the saltwater lagoons, eating the dead vegetation and plankton.

We drove slowly past the shallow bayou where fishing enthusiasts were happily catching fish in the warm shallow waters or crabbing with a dip net. There are a couple of canoe launch sites but motorized boats are prohibited in order to protect the seagrass beds and their aquatic residents.

Wading birds take advantage of the horseshoe sandbars to catch small fish and we saw several ospreys skimming the water and cleaning their fishy talons on the sandy bed.

There are many occupied osprey nests throughout the refuge. The best time to see birds is during the migratory season but even in April we saw a reddish egret, some unusual red-breasted merganser ducks, cormorants, a yellow-crowned night heron, willets, mottled ducks and a beautiful white pelican.

The tram tour stops by the boardwalk at Red Mangrove Overlook and our guide was soon pointing out a snake and several black tree crabs on the branches and tangled prop roots of the mangroves. The lagoon has a sandy bottom which makes it easy to spot lightning whelks using their "foot" to move around and feed. There are many tiny fish and shoals of large mullet that can be seen jumping out of the water and landing on their sides, This is thought to blow air out of their gills in order to remove the parasites and detritus that accumulate there.

Further along Wildlife Drive we stopped to see fiddler crabs waving their claws. Horseshoe crabs with their hard shells and long tails were swimming in the brown water which is caused by tannins leaching from the mangroves.

At the end of the Wildlife Drive, the tour returns to the car park via the Sanibel-Captiva Road.

Additional Info

Other activities available in the "Ding" Darling Natural Wildlife Refuge include hiking and cycling along the rough road. You can bring your own bicycle or rent one. Kayaking, paddleboard tours, nature and sea-life cruises, fishing charters and boat rentals can all be arranged through Tarpon Bay Explorers' office on the "Ding" Darling Refuge car park.

Dogs are allowed on the Wildlife Drive provided they are kept on a short leash.

Binoculars are very useful for watching the birds and wildlife.

Admission
Visitor Center - Free

Wildlife Drive
Motorized vehicle $5
Hiker/biker $1
Children 15 and under Free

Tram Tours
Adults $13
Children $8

Opening Times

"Ding" Darling Wildlife Drive

Saturday to Thursday 7.30 a.m. to 7 p.m.
The Wildlife Drive is closed Fridays to all public access. This is to allow for any maintenance and to give the wildlife a chance to feed with no human disturbance.

"Ding" Darling Visitor Center

January to April 9 a.m. to 5 p.m. daily
May to December 9 a.m. to 4 p.m. daily
Closed most Federal holidays

Tram Tour Times

Saturday to Thursday 8 a.m.to 6 p.m. hourly

Where to Eat Near the "Ding" Darling Wildlife Refuge

The Green Flash Restaurant is highly recommended and is on the adjoining Captiva Island. It offers casual dining and has a good reputation for its fish and seafood. A popular restaurant for boaters, it has indoor and outdoor dining and great waterfront views.

The Lighthouse Café on Periwinkle Way boasts the world's best breakfast and is well worth a visit for lunch too. Dinner is also available from December to April.

Nearby Attractions

- Bailey-Matthews Shell Museum
- Sanibel Historical Museum and Village
- Bowman's Beach
- Sanibel Lighthouse

Bailey-Matthews Shell Museum

One of Sanibel Island's most interesting attractions is the Bailey-Matthews Shell Museum, considered the most comprehensive museum in the western hemisphere for shells. It is a most appropriate natural history attraction as Sanibel is considered one of the world's top shelling destinations. As well as a huge collection of seashells from all over the world, the museum includes a hands-on children's learning lab, informative videos in the theater, workshops, live tanks of living mollusks and 35 labeled exhibits including a life-size recreation of the Native American Calusa Indians, the original residents of Sanibel.

Rated a "Gem" attraction by AAA, the Shell Museum is an ideal attraction for families with children and anyone interested in natural history. The museum sponsors a field trip program for Lee County School pupils through the Adopt-a-Class scheme and has the distinction of being one of the few museums in the USA to earn the American Alliance of Museums (AAM) accreditation for their high standards of excellence.

The Shell Museum is very much a local treasure, started with a donation by Charlene McMurphy of Sanibel and incorporated as a non-profit museum in 1986. The donation of a parcel of land four years later by the Bailey family in memory of their parents, Frank P. Bailey and Annie Mead Matthews, gave the museum a permanent home and a new name. The museum is an integral part of the Sanibel community and is one of the island's main attractions.

Location
4 miles west of Sanibel Causeway Bridge

3075 Sanibel-Captiva Road
Sanibel
FL33957
Tel: (239) 395-2233

www.shellmuseum.org

GPS Coordinates: 26.43821,-82.092886

Directions

After crossing the toll bridge onto Sanibel Island, head west along Periwinkle Way and follow the signs for Captiva. After joining Sanibel-Captiva Road, the Shell Museum is about ½ mile on the left.

What to Expect at the Shell Museum

Located in a purpose-built octagonal building on Sanibel-Captiva Road, the well-established Shell Museum is a delightful and informative attraction for all ages. The main reception area is at the top of a flight of steps and has a display of various shell pictures and murals around the walls.

There is a wealth of informative literature you can pick up here, including a shell identification card in full color, an interesting brochure about Alphabet Cones, information sheets about the history of the Bailey-Matthews Shell Museum, facts and myths about sea shells and tips for shell seekers on where and when to find the best shells.

Move into the spacious well-lit Great Hall of Shells which has over 30 exhibits and displays in purpose-built glass cases and freestanding units located all around the octagonal-shaped room. The beautifully arranged displays of shells are from all over the world with a special section dedicated to shells found in southwest Florida. Wall-mounted glass cases house shells in their particular family groups.

Look out for the beautiful display of Sailors' Valentines - octagonal boxes filled with tiny shells arranged in solid patterns to create a beautiful keepsake. These skillful works of art included personal messages written in shells, They were made in the 19th century by women in Barbados and the Caribbean to sell to visiting sailors.

Another fantastic example of shell-art was the display of cameos beautifully carved into large Emperor's Helmet Shells. Other uses of shells included the making of buttons and bows and the abalone interior is often used in costume jewelry. Shells in architecture; rare, beautiful and unusual specimens and a shell classification wheel all have their place in this well-laid-out exhibit space.

Rare samples of cone shells, colorful scallop shells and some record-breaking large shells were available to view and read about along with cowrie shells which were used as an early form of currency. During my visit, a school party was on a guided tour learning about how some mollusks could be lethal while others have a beneficial role to play in medicine. Another corner that was clearly popular with younger visitors was the Children's Learning Lab with hands-on displays, a shell specimen cabinet and a live pool of mollusks.

The Museum Auditorium offers two 30-minute videos played back to back. *Mollusks in Action* was followed by *Trails and Tales of Living Seashells and Other Sea Creatures*. Text subtitles made it easy to understand as the film followed the different trails made in the sand by various mollusks. It also identified the different parts of the live mollusk which were used for movement and for eating. Live sand dollars and sea stars were among other marine creatures featured in the films.

Last stop was in the Museum Store which has an attractive selection of shell-themed goods from home accents and shell-design napkins to tasteful T-shirts, vases, tableware, photo frames, books, jewelry and other tempting souvenir items.

Additional Info

Taking a guided tour will greatly add to the informative value of any visit. Guided and private tours are offered to groups of all ages and reservations are required ahead of time. Tours are free with the price of admission.

Admission

Adults $9
Youths 5-16 $5
Children 4 and under Free

Opening Times

Daily 10 a.m. to 5 p.m.
Closed New Year's Day, Easter, July 4th, Thanksgiving and Christmas Day.

Where to Eat near the Bailey-Matthews Shell Museum

Sanibel has a huge choice of places to eat. Try the Greenhouse Grill on Periwinkle Way which is within easy reach by bicycle, car or on foot from the Shell Museum. Doc Ford's Rum Bar and Grill on the corner of Rabbit Road is another favorite gathering place on Sanibel. Try their banana leaf snapper cooked the island way with a tangy Mojito to wash it down.

Nearby Attractions
- J.N. "Ding" Darling National Wildlife Refuge
- Sanibel Lighthouse
- Bowmans Beach
- Captiva Island

Six Mile Cypress Slough Preserve

The Six Mile Cypress Slough, pronounced "slew," is a 2,500-acre natural wetland preserve with a pleasant boardwalk traversing this forested wetland area. Visitors can visit the preserve, take a guided walk with a wildlife specialist and learn about local wildlife and the importance of this freshwater wetlands ecosystem.

With an informative interpretive Center and free Explorer's Companion booklet, visitors can spots birds and animals from the 1.2 mile-long boardwalk. Identify trees, gaze out on lakes and ponds from constructed viewing platforms and a hide as you stroll along a boardwalk that continually twists and turns through greenery.

Apt quotations, 31 numbered points of interest and recreated animals tracks on the boardwalk make this a pleasant area of recreation for all ages and fitness levels.

The Six Mile Cypress Slough Preserve is a linear ecosystem 9 miles long and 1/3 mile wide. The Pine Flatwoods, shady hardwood area, hammocks and ponds are home to many plants and animals, some of which are considered endangered.

Discover more about natural Florida with a visit to this peaceful area and keep your eyes moving to spot grey squirrels, pileated woodpeckers, nesting birds, egrets, ibis, herons as well as the more elusive bobcats, raccoons, wild boar and playful river otters.

Location
Located on Six Mile Cypress Parkway, south of Winkler and 1.5 miles north of Daniels Parkway.

7751 Penzance Blvd
Fort Myers
Tel: (239) 533-7550

GPS Coordinates: 26.5705, -81.8260

http://www.leeparks.org/sixmile/index.html

Directions

Take exit 131 off I-75 and head west along Daniel's Parkway to Six Mile Cypress Pkwy.

Turn right and drive north 1.5 miles to Penzance Blvd before turning right into the preserve.

Things to Do at Six Mile Cypress Slough Preserve

After parking and purchasing a parking ticket, your first visit should definitely start in the Interpretive Center. Browse the well-presented exhibit and chat with the staff who will be happy to help you make the most of your visit. Just outside on a broad raised deck there are a collection of rocking chairs which make the perfect place to listen to the local wildlife, or to "take five" before setting out on the boardwalk trail.

Guided tours with a wildlife specialist are a wonderful way to be introduced to Six Mile Cypress Slough Preserve. They take place daily at 9.30 a.m. and 1.30 p.m. from January through March, daily at 9.30 a.m. in April, November, and December, and Wednesdays only from May to October, again at 9.30 a.m. Just turn up and join the group at the head of the boardwalk.

If you are walking the path independently, you can pick up a helpful Explorer's Companion booklet from the box just after the restrooms at the start of the boardwalk trail. These brochures give information on each of the numbered points of interest along the way. At the end, visitors are asked to return the guide to the box for other visitors to use.

The well-constructed boardwalk is superbly designed to zigzag around the tall trees and is never straight or boring. Along the way there are seating areas, shelters and observation decks over the ponds and places of particular interest. There is a photo blind overlooking the final pond, Pop Ash Pond, where otters, turtles and herons can be viewed undisturbed.

The sights and sounds of nature are all around and visitors are advised to walk slowly and quietly, watching and listening for movement. Wildlife is out there, with many eyes watching you and your patience will be rewarded with some wonderful sighting and photo opportunities. If you have binoculars you will be able to view nesting birds in spring on the opposite banks of Gator Lake.

In the dry season you will find boggy mud just below the boardwalk, which is great for spotting animal tracks. However, in the wet season from June to November, the area is covered in 2-3 feet of water with hammocks of greenery, the swollen trunks of cypress trees and the tops of their "knees" just breaking the surface. By the way, river otters can look very much like cypress knees, so do look closely, just in case!

Although the boardwalk offers flat, easy walking you should allow at least an hour to complete the full walk. If you want to enjoy a shorter walk, the lower loop is just 0.75 mile. Fascinating in all seasons, the Six Mile Cypress Slough Preserve is a valuable local resource which continues to provide a home and corridor for wildlife, a quiet place for visitors to enjoy the peace of wildlife, and a great place to take a walk and enjoy some fresh air.

Additional Info

The Six Mile Cypress Slough was rescued from logging by a group of local residents known simply as the Monday Group. Concerned by how the forested wetlands of Florida were disappearing, they highlighted the plight of the slough. Lee County residents were spurred into action and increased their own local taxes to purchase the land and create a preserve as an oasis for plants, animals and local visitors to enjoy. In 1991 Lee County Parks and Recreation opened the superb boardwalk, providing access and facilities to create this prime recreational area and natural preserve.

Admission

Free admission.
Parking is $1 per hour

Opening Times

Dawn to dusk daily
Interpretive Center is open:
November to April Tues – Sat 10 a.m. to 4 p.m.; Sunday 10 a.m. to 2 p.m.
May to October Tues – Sunday 10 a.m. to 2 p.m.

Where to Eat at Six Mile Cypress Slough Preserve

Picnic areas and seating areas make this the perfect place to enjoy a picnic, so come prepared!

Nearby Attractions

- Edison Ford Winter Estates
- Burroughs Home and Gardens
- TrueTours Historical Walking Tours
- Koreshan State Park

Calusa Nature Center and Planetarium

The Calusa Nature Center and Planetarium is run as a non-profit educational attraction which includes three nature trails, a museum, a walk-through butterfly enclosure, several aviaries and a planetarium. Spread over 105 acres, it is a great way for visitors and residents to learn more about the native wildlife and birds in southwest Florida, especially through the daily animal presentations and educational programs.

Founded in 1976, the Calusa Nature Center has a Natural History Living Museum with a selection of wildlife. It is home to the Audubon Aviary, a sanctuary for injured birds, including bald eagles, hawks, owls and a cage of noisy vultures. The Calusa Nature Center Planetarium is the only one open to the public in southwest Florida.

Arrive early and plan your time around the scheduled Planetarium shows and activities presented by the resident animal handler to get the most from your visit. There are Live Reptile Presentations, Meet the Mammals, Alligator Feedings and Snake Feedings at various times and locations.

Describing itself as "The Eco Place with Outer Space", there's more to the Calusa Nature Center and Planetarium than you might think!

Location
The Nature Center is located at the intersection of Colonial Blvd and Ortiz Ave/Six Mile Cypress Blvd.

3450 Ortiz Ave
Fort Myers
FL33905
Tel: (239) 275-3435

www.calusanature.org/

GPS Coordinates: 26.61576,-81.81222

Directions
From I-75 take exit 136 and go west on Colonial Blvd. ¼ mile to Ortiz Ave.

Turn right onto Ortiz Ave and the entrance to the center is 500 feet along on the left.

What to Expect at the Calusa Nature Center and Planetarium

Your visit starts at the Visitor Center where there is a natural history museum with a good selection of exhibits and interpretive displays. The touch tank of mollusks is sure to fascinate curious young visitors.

Moving outdoors along the paths, there are plenty of Florida residents waiting to greet you including a coyote, a red fox, bobcat, otter, black bear and raccoons in the natural enclosures. The water feature is home to various reptiles, turtles and amphibious creatures.

Guided walks with a naturalist are available at certain times and live animals shows presenting iguanas and other creatures are an interesting way to learn more about Florida animals.

More wildlife can be seen up close in the Audubon Aviary including bald eagles, red-tailed hawks, broad-winged hawks, red-shouldered hawks, owls and a cage of noisy vultures. Enter the butterfly aviary and admire the gorgeous colors and fluttering butterflies as they flit from one plant to the next, collecting nectar.

The peaceful bird garden has a seat for watching birds at the bird feeders and a memory walk. Another interesting feature is the young oak tree, grown from an acorn of the historic oak tree which stood in front of the Lee County Courthouse in downtown Fort Myers.

The extensive grounds are given over to native Florida greenery with many saw palms, ferns, sabal palm trees and vines. Bat boxes and nesting boxes encourage local wildlife to breed in this peaceful sanctuary.

Visitors have the option of a ⅓ mile Pine Loop Trail or diverting off along the ½ mile-long Cypress Boardwalk. The trails wind through the greenery with the occasional cypress knees creating a tripping hazard. The longest Wild Lands Trail runs around the property for 1.3 miles.

The area is home to many native birds and wildlife and you may spot animals or their tracks along the sandy trail. The walks all have a series of numbered information boards identifying various trees and plants.

The Planetarium is 44 feet in diameter and seats up to 87 people with 3 wheelchair spaces. There are usually two full-dome planetarium shows each day with films highlighting various seasonal constellations and how to locate them.

It also shows updates of the latest space missions such as Mars exploration, the Keplar Mission and the NASA Science Laboratory Missions. Visitors can gaze at the sun through a special solar telescope or watch highlights of previous Space Shuttle projects.

The Gift Shop has various types of natural history-themed merchandise for sale along with books, gifts and jewelry.

The Calusa Nature Center and Planetarium has an impressive schedule of presentations so it is worth checking the times of events for the day you plan to visit by calling (239) 275-3435. Guided walks with a naturalist, reptile programs, planetarium shows and Dog Day Sundays all add to the fun of any visit.

Additional Info

Guided walks along the Cypress Swamp Boardwalk are led by a volunteer docent every Tuesday and Friday (excluding the last Friday in the month).

The Calusa Nature Center has a varied program of activities throughout the year such as Scavenger Hunts, Night Hikes, the Laser Lights Show in April, Haunted Lights, the Holiday Arbor Lights and the Annual Creepy Crawlie Day.

Evening lectures by guest speakers are offered from time to time in the planetarium.

Admission

Adults $10
Children 3-12 $5
Discounts for seniors, students, active military and AAA members

Opening Times

Monday-Saturday 10 a.m. to 5 p.m.; Sunday 11 a.m. to 5 p.m.

Where to Eat near the Calusa Nature Center

There are plenty of seats and places to enjoy a picnic as part of your visit to Calusa Nature Center and Planetarium.

Nearby Colonial Boulevard has many fast food restaurants such as Bob Evans, McDonalds and Chick-fil-A. The El Gaucho Inca Restaurant has a good reputation for steak and seafood at moderate prices.

Nearby Attractions
- Lakes Park
- Six Mile Cypress Slough Preserve
- Imaginarium
- Southwest Florida Museum of History

Koreshan State Historic Site

The Koreshan State Historic Site is a very unique and interesting place to visit. It is the preserved site of a 19th century religious community with 11 original buildings, Victorian gardens, a nature trail along the Estero River, canoeing and camp sites in a 200-acre park.

Self-guided tour leaflets and information boards are available, along with volunteer docents, for those who want to tour the grounds at their own pace. However, I can recommend taking a 90-minute ranger-led tour for those wanting to delve into the beliefs of Dr. Cyrus Teed and understand the day-to-day operations of his "New Jerusalem".

Koreshanity began in Estero in 1893 and lasted until 1982 when the last member died. Along with tours, the historic estate hosts the Estero Concert Series which attracts professional musicians and world class opera singers to perform in the atmospheric Art Hall. It also offers re-enactments and ghost walks at Halloween which are well worth attending.

Location
Koreshan is located at the intersection of US 41 and Corkscrew Road at Estero.

3800 Corkscrew Road
Estero
FL33928
Tel: (239) 992-0311

www.floridastateparks.org/koreshan/

http://mwweb.org/koreshan/blog/

GPS Coordinates: 26.433257, -81.814653

Directions
From I-75, take exit 123 (Corkscrew Road) and head west 2 miles.

Cross US 41 and continue along Corkscrew Road about ½ mile to reach the entrance to the park.

What to Expect on a Walking Tour

At the entrance ranger station, pay the admission and book a place on the next guided tour if you want a ranger-led experience of the historic site and gardens. The tour meets just off the car park outside the Art Hall, where a huge swamp mahogany provides shade from the Florida sun.

The tour begins in the beautiful Art Hall which is still used for public concerts as in the days of the Koreshan Unity Settlement. The hall is filled with artworks by former Koreshan members and by Dr. Teed's son, Douglas Arthur Teed, who became a well-known landscape and portrait artist in New York.

The most remarkable exhibit is the globe which shows the world as we know it, but on the inner shell of the earth's outer atmosphere, as Dr. Teed believed it was.

We followed our knowledgeable volunteer guide, Mila, along the crushed shell paths passing Orchid Trees in full bloom, a Sabal Palm with cacti growing on the trunk, and finally reached the cherry orchard just outside the Planetary Court building.

Here we learnt more about Dr. Teed and his "illumination" in 1869 which led him to Chicago and then to Estero to found his Koreshan Unity, the word "Koreshan" being Persian for "shepherd". His new order followed a mix of Old Testament, Far Eastern ideas, reincarnation and Teed's own scientific beliefs. His ultimate aim was to define the universe through science.

About 3,000 members lived outside the settlement with their families while up to 300 others chose to join the religious order at Koreshan, which required giving their property to the community and living celibate lives onsite.

The followers were hard-working people and the community was self-sufficient, even providing services to the outside community. They valued education and the arts and had their own drama group and 17-piece orchestra which performed public concerts.

The three-story Planetary Court is a fine example of Georgia Foursquare architecture, built in 1904. The cream clapboard house with its shady front porch was home to the Seven "Sisters", They provided much of the original finance Teed required to establish his community and saw to the day-to-day business of the settlement.

Each lady had her own simply furnished room and a caretaker looked after them and lived at the top of the house, in the cupola. Check out the ornate craftsman-built staircase made of beautiful date pine. There are no baths or kitchen in the house as the Sisters ate formally each evening at the communal dining area.

All the buildings are on the National Register of Historic Places, but there was never a church on site. The bakery once made up to 600 loaves a day – the yeast bread was in great demand locally as it was so much tastier than the local cornbread.

Other buildings include the two-room Vesta Newcombe building, final home to Vesta who arrived at the community as a child and lived here until her death in her 90s.

There is an industrial area with a huge oil-driven generator which once powered the band saws and machinery in the neighboring machine shops as well as providing power to the surrounding outlying farms.

The Koreshan Unity was totally dependent upon Dr. Teed and after his death in 1908 many followers became disillusioned when his teachings about his resurrection were not fulfilled. Eventually the Koreshan community, its archives and substantial acreage were donated to the state of Florida, in 1961.

The final part of the tour takes you through the gardens where there are many specimen trees sourced by Dr. Teed on his travels all over the world. Look for the huge Australian Monkey Puzzle Tree, the exotic flowers on the Bombax (red silk cotton tree), the Ear Tree and the African Sausage Tree. Fruit trees, pecans, magnolias and lovely red pineapples with their exotic pink fruits can be enjoyed as well as more common azaleas and palms.

Landscaped mounds make a popular place for the burrowing Gopher Tortoises and two decorative bridges are an interesting highlight. Massive Washingtonian Palms planted in 1896 line the Grande Promenade which is visible from the Bamboo Landing.

Here you are likely to see canoeists paddling in the clear shallow waters of the Estero River, which was the main access to the settlement before US41 was paved. This area is the start of the Nature Trail, a pleasant 30-minute walk along the river, through immense bamboo stands and the picnic area to end at the boat ramp. Having done it, I would recommend going out and back along the river trail which is a much more pleasant than returning on the park roads. Otters, herons, bobcats, foxes, alligators, snakes and a variety of birds of prey all make their home in the park.

Our tour ended at the Founders House, built for Cyrus Teed in 1896 and surprisingly comfortably furnished. There is an interesting display of old photographs of the Koreshan community in its heyday and an informative PBS film gives more background detail to this short-lived religious sect.

Additional Info
There is an excellent Guide to the Koreshan Unity Settlement with a brief history, map of historic area and details of each building.

The Self-guided Tour of the Gardens brochure is also filled with information and has a numbered plan of the main specimen plants and trees.

Both these brochures are available from a display box as you walk along the concrete footpath from the car park to the Art Hall. Suggested donations of 50c per brochure are requested.

Admission
Park Admission
$2 for walkers and cyclists
$4 per vehicle and up to 8 passengers

Guided Walking Tour
$2 per adult; $1 for under 12s

Canoe hire
$5 per hour; $25 for the day
Canoe Rentals are handled at the Entrance Ranger Station

Opening Times
The park is open 8 a.m. to sundown daily

Guided Walking Tours of the Historic Site
January - March these guided tours take place at 10 a.m. and 2 p.m. daily.
April - December at 10 a.m. Saturdays and Sundays only
Guided tours can also be scheduled in advance on request.

Where to Eat near Koreshan State Historic Site
Estero has a number of family-run restaurants which finish off your visit to Koreshan perfectly. Cocina Mexicana El Tenampa is a husband and wife Mexican restaurant on South Tamiami Trail which is renowned for its quesadillas and delicious Texas burritos.

Just down the road from Koreshan is the award-winning Tony Sacco's Coal Oven Pizza on Plaza del Lago Drive, or try Hemingway's Island Grill for great handcrafted "island" food at the same location.

Nearby Attractions
- Lakes Park
- Six Mile Cypress Slough Preserve
- Corkscrew Swamp Sanctuary

Fort Myers Beach

No visit to the Fort Myers area is complete without a day or two on Fort Myers Beach. Most visitors head straight for the beach to relax with a good book, go swimming in the calm Gulf waters, walk along the firm sands or go shelling along the water's edge. The area also offers boat trips and fishing charters, bike and paddleboard rentals, adventure golf, guided nature kayak tours and sunset cruises. You can even take a trip to Key West or spend the day on a Casino Cruise from this popular resort.

Beach chairs and umbrellas are available for hire on the beach along with waverunners and parasailing. The area has four parks including the inlets and islands in Estero Bay Preserve State Park, the Matanzas Pass Preserve, Bowditch

Point Park and the tiny Lynn Hall Memorial Park with a playground, picnic shelters and a fishing pier.

With plenty of Florida sunshine, a refreshing breeze and a good choice of restaurants and facilities near the pier, Fort Myers Beach is a perfect day out for families and beach lovers of all ages.

Location

15 miles south of Downtown Fort Myers on the barrier island of Estero

www.fortmyersbeachfl.gov/

GPS Coordinates: 26.452255,-81.947639

Directions

From I-75 Exit 131, or US-41 follow Daniels Parkway/Cypress Lake Drive west to Summerlin Road.

Turn left and follow the road southwest to San Carlos Blvd (FL-865). Turn left and follow the highway over the bridge until you reach Estero Blvd.

Turn right for Bowditch Point Park or follow the main route to the left and drive along Estero Blvd parallel to the beach to find parking.

Things to Do at Fort Myers Beach

Fort Myers Beach lies almost 15 miles south of downtown Fort Myers. Once San Carlos Blvd reaches Fort Myers Beach, it meets Estero Blvd which runs in either direction parallel to the beach.

On this corner, if you follow the main route and bend sharp left at Times Square, the road runs along the barrier island of Estero for about six miles before crossing the bridge and entering Lovers Key State Park. Alternatively, if you turn right, Times Square offers parking and there is a playground for children, volleyball courts, cafés, ice cream parlors and beach shops nearby.

The road in this westerly direction ends after one mile at Bowditch Point Recreational Park which has picnic tables, walking trails, watersports and is a great place to watch the sunset. Locals tell me that when the Key West Express passes Bowditch Point around 8.30 a.m. daily, huge numbers of dolphins play in the wake, leaping fully out of the water in a wonderful display that may last 15-20 minutes.

The town of Fort Myers Beach has around 6,000 permanent residents and many more temporary visitors throughout the year. The beachfront is lined with beach homes of all sizes and styles, along with low-rise vacation condos, several churches, shops, restaurants, shopping plazas and motels.

Beach parking at Fort Myers Beach is available in a number of car parks with metered spaces, or in private car parks where daily charges range upwards from $6. Close to the fishing pier are the main attractions clustered around the Lani Kai Island Resort which has restrooms, beachfront cafés and a rooftop restaurant. In the winter season there are rows of umbrellas and chair rentals along with waverunners, banana boat rides and parasailing watersports. The Gulf waters are shallow, calm and warm, making it ideal for families to enjoy a day on the beach.

Fort Myers Beach has exceptionally firm sand for walking or cycling at low tide. It is also the perfect consistency for sandsculpting and making sandcastles. Every year in late November, Fort Myers Beach hosts the American Sandsculpting Championships and visitors can buy tickets to see a range of large-scale sand sculptures.

The beach is always littered with seashells, from large lightning whelks and fighting conchs to sand dollars and tiny rose pink tellins. Shell collecting is a popular pastime for visitors. However, some shells may still have living creatures inside them, so do check they are empty before popping them into your bag.

As you head further south, the beach becomes increasingly less commercialized and crowded. There is a paddle craft landing, walking trails and guided nature walks for exploring the wilderness sanctuary at Matanzas Pass Preserve.

Boat Trips from Fort Myers Beach

For more adventure, several boat trips are offered from Fort Myers Beach. How about a day in the beautiful Caribbean paradise of Key West? Sail aboard the *Key West Express* passenger catamaran which departs daily at 8.30 a. returning at 9.30 p.m. The journey each way takes 3½ hours and gives visitors a whole six hours in this laid-back island paradise. The boat trip offers great coastal and sea views, and the chance to spot dolphins. There is a sundeck, snack bar and cocktails as well as big screen TVs so getting there is half the fun!

Alternatively, take a Casino Cruise on the luxurious 162-foot *Big M* which includes bingo, dancing, casino tables, slots and an optional all-you-can-eat buffet. Choose from an all-day cruise Wednesday through Sunday 10.30 a.m. to 4.30 p.m. or a party cruise on Friday and Saturdays nights from 6 p.m. to 11.45 p.m.

Additional Info
Fishing Charters at Fort Myers Beach
Fort Myers Fishing Adventures
2500 Main Street
Fort Myers Beach
(239) 896-6635

Capt. Richard Cain's Dock
18650 San Carlos Blvd
Fort Myers Beach
(239) 590 0990

Catch Me If U Can Fishing Charters
50 Estero Blvd
Fort Myers Beach
(239)210-8339

Bike, Kayak, Paddleboard & Watersports Rentals

Fun-n-Sun Bike and Paddleboard Rentals
Local delivery service
(239) 728-7564

LK Paddleboard Rentals
1400 Estero Blvd
Fort Myers Beach
(239) 463-3111

Mid-Island Watersports
5550 Estero Blvd
Fort Myers Beach
(239) 765-0965

Paradise Parasail
1160 Estero Blvd
Fort Myers Beach
(239) 463-7272

Boat Charters, Sunset and Dolphin Cruises

Sunset Ride Private Charters
18400 San Carlos Blvd
Fort Myers Beach
(239) 839-2109

Good Time Charters
7225 Estero Blvd
Fort Myers Beach
(239) 437-8773

The Big M Casino Cruises
450 Harbor Court
Fort Myers Beach (239) 765-PLAY

Key West Express
1200 Main Street
Fort Myers Beach
(239) 463-5733 or (888) 539-2628

Where to Eat near Fort Myers Beach
Start the day at the Island Pancake House at the Sea Grape Plaza on Estero Blvd before strolling across the highway to the beach.

The Lani Kai Island Resort is the focal point for entertainment on the beach and it has hot dogs, milkshakes and beach snacks available from Mario's Deli and the Chicago Dog House. The fabulous rooftop setting of the Island View Restaurant is unrivalled, overlooking the beach, and the swinging glider seats are fun. The menu has a good choice of American favorites, pasta dishes, salads and steaks. The Prime Rib is an excellent deal! Parking fees are refunded against your meal.

For fresh seafood, try the Beach Seafood Market on 1100 Shrimp Boat Lane. As well as having a fresh fish shop right where the fishing fleet unload, there is a lunchtime all-you-can-eat seafood buffet in the café which is excellent value.

Nervous Nellies on First Street is a casual family restaurant with a great reputation for its food. It has a full bar and live music at Ugly's upstairs and you can't beat the waterfront views from the deck.

Nearby Attractions

- Lakes Regional Park
- Koreshan Historic State Park
- Corkscrew Swamp Sanctuary
- Bailey-Mathews Shell Museum
- J.N."Ding" Darling Nature Wildlife Refuge

Corkscrew Swamp Sanctuary

Located in the Western Everglades, Corkscrew Swamp Sanctuary and the Blair Audubon Center provide an amazing and informative experience of native Florida wildlife.

The 13,000 acre wildlife preserve takes its name from the Corkscrew River (now known as the Imperial River) which meanders with deep twists and turns through the region. The National Audubon Society has protected the area as a bird sanctuary since 1912 and it is home to over 200 species of birds.

During the 1940s and 50s when native cypress trees were being felled at an alarming rate, it became apparent that this area needed to be further protected as a conservation area and wildlife habitat.

In 1954, 14 separate organizations joined with the National Audubon Society and the first area of swamp and cypress was purchased. At that time the area was almost inaccessible, so a boardwalk was built enabling visitors to enjoy the birds and wildlife without having any impact on the environment.

Location
20 miles east of Bonita Springs off CR 846.

375 Sanctuary Road West
Naples
FL34120
Tel: (239) 348-9151

www.corkscrew.audubon.org/

GPS Co-ordinates: 26.374492,-81.60541

Directions
From I-75 take exit 111 and head east on Immokalee Road (CR-846).

After 15 miles, turn left onto Sanctuary Road and after ¾ mile turn left into Sanctuary Road W. The entrance to the Corkscrew Swamp Sanctuary is in 1 mile where the road meets Rookery Lane.

What to Expect at Corkscrew Swamp Sanctuar

Visitors will find that the Corkscrew Swamp Sanctuary covers six distinct areas of different habitat: Bald Cypress, Pond Cypress, Wet Prairie, Sawgrass Pond, Pine Flatwood, and Central Marsh, all easily viewed from the shady 2¼ mile-long boardwalk.

First stop is at the Blair Audubon Center where information, a nature store, café and exhibits can be seen. Purchase your admission ticket here before heading into the theater for a 14-minute informative sound and light presentation. Visitors stand in the theater and learn a little about the wildlife they are about to see. Listen to the bird calls, the growl of an alligator and the strange barks of tree frogs as the presentation highlights the various residents of this reserve. You can hire binoculars for $3 or pick up a free stroller or wheelchair to enhance your visit.

The boardwalk is made of sustainable pau-lope hardwood which blends into the natural scenery as it is covered in patches of lichen. Although the full length of the boardwalk circuit is over 2 miles, there is a shortcut to return along a shorter loop if required.

It is fascinating to stroll along within touching distance of ancient bald cypress, palms, ferns, flowering shrubs, and marsh plants. If you stop to look carefully, the marsh plants are covered in tiny white, yellow, red and blue flowers which can easily be missed, so do take your time!

With the help of the Companion Field Guide to the reserve ($2) it is fun to identify pickerelweed, broad leaved arrowheads, buttonbush, water dropwort, and even the solitary red bloom of an enormous swamp hibiscus. Air plants (epiphytes) are perched in tree crevices and in one area strangler figs can be seen creating a sturdy support network on their chosen host tree.

Bird song, insect noises, twitters and shrieks add natural background noise. The sound carries over the still wetland, so do be aware that your voice can be heard far away too! We heard a woodpecker hammering into the top of a huge cypress tree and the squawks and grunts of vultures squabbling over a tasty kill. Bright orange Ruddy Daggerwing butterflies flit around, clearly in butterfly paradise, and we saw hairy caterpillars, wading birds and many spiders on their perfectly formed webs.

If I sound incredibly knowledgeable, then I'll let you into a secret. The boardwalk is patrolled by rangers who are happy to stop, answer questions, and identify flowers and creatures. They also walk the boardwalk adding temporary signs to the balustrades pointing out the web of a spotted orb weaver, or a black and yellow argiope spider with its long black and yellow banded legs. These useful signs helped us to spot nesting sites, a yellow rat snake sleeping in the hole of a tree and a rare ghost orchid high in another one. There are also a series of interpretive boards giving bite-sized chunks of information as you walk.

Rangers have a selection of exhibits that draw quite a crowd. Visitors can hold a young alligator, see a hollow alligator tooth, and learn about why the alligator has bumps on its back.

The gentle amble around with detours to viewpoints and the Marsh Observation Platform takes 1-2 hours, depending on how many plants and creatures you want to stop and photograph, but it is a wonderfully pleasant walk. Even if you visit on a sunny day (I visited in October when it was still 90°F), there is plenty of shade and a gentle breeze at times.

Finish your visit and support this wonderful charity further by having drinks or a snack in the café and browsing the excellent range of books and gifts in the nature store.

Additional Info

You may want to return to Corkscrew Swamp Sanctuary and join one of their monthly Corkscrew After Hours evening projects which have a theme of bats, bird migration, stargazing and other topics.

The After Hours Project offers a walk in this ancient forest with a totally different perspective from a daytime visit. Specialists are brought in to enhance the educational experience, with equipment such as telescopes and a bat detector to listen as the bats forage and feed. Hear hooting owls, croaking frogs, identify planets and stars, and spot the glowing amber eyes of alligators under a bright moon.

There is no additional cost beyond the regular admission price. Simply turn up between 6.45 and 9pm on selected dates and learn something new!

Admission (valid for 2 consecutive days)
Adults $12
Students (3-18) $6

Opening Times
Daily 7 a.m. to 5.30 p.m.
Monthly Corkscrew After Hours Event until 9 p.m.

Where to Eat at Corkscrew Swamp Sanctuary
The onsite tearoom has indoor and outdoor seating for visitors to enjoy refreshments. It offers fresh sandwiches and salads supplied daily by Taste Buds Custom Catering.

If you prefer to bring your own picnic, there are picnic tables in the car park area.

Nearby Attractions
- Naples Zoo
- Fort Myers Beach
- Koreshan State Historic Site

Naples Zoo at Caribbean Gardens

Naples Zoo is one of the top attractions in southwest Florida. Although not extensive, the 52-acre gardens are the ideal size to explore even on the hottest day. The shady paths weave around the naturalized enclosures with floor-to-ceiling clear glass viewing areas for little ones. Florida black bears, zebra, lions and a collection of rare animals and reptiles can all be enjoyed within a pleasant tropical garden setting.

Naples Zoo has some very unique attractions such as feeding the giraffes and riding a camel for a small additional fee, and these activities really makes this zoo particularly fun and memorable. A 20-minute boat ride takes visitors around the ape-inhabited islands which is a nice rest for aching feet. Show times, Feeding Times and Meet the Keeper events provide information and education along with the chance to get up-close to the local inhabitants. Ample picnic tables, clear signs, plenty of food and drinks stands and a good size Gift Shop make this a well-planned attraction providing a most enjoyable day out for all ages.

Location
Naples Zoo is off US-41/ I-75, just north of Naples and opposite the Coastland Center Mall. It is 14 miles south of Bonita Springs.

1590 Goodlette-Frank Rd
Naples
FL 34102
Tel: (239) 262-5409

www.napleszoo.org

GPS Coordinates: 26.1697, -81.7889

Directions
From I-75 take exit 105 (Golden Gate Parkway) and drive west towards the beach. After 4 miles turn left (south) on Goodlette-Frank Road. The zoo parking and entrance is on the left opposite the Coastland Center Mall.

OR: From US-41 turn east into Fleishmann Blvd and cross Goodlette-Frank Road into the parking area.

Things to Do at Naples Zoo

Naples Zoo is fairly small and easy to cover in a day. It is a collection of rare animals in a shady tropical garden setting with a number of large, easily recognizable animals including giraffes, zebra, lions, monkeys, big cats, alligators, gazelle, antelopes, wallabies and Florida black bears. They all have generously sized enclosures with naturalized vegetation and clear floor-to-ceiling windows for youngsters to get a good view of the more interesting animals. The bears even have a huge ice cube to scratch, drink and play with in hot weather.

The zoo also has numerous smaller creatures such as honey badgers, beautiful red and green macaws, porcupines and insects. There are plenty of relatively unknown animals and rare species too. Some of the most fascinating creatures are in the glass-fronted displays near the admission desk in the Gift Shop and they are worth looking out for. They included the mossy toad and some very unusual colored frogs and insects.

At the admission desk, visitors receive a map of the zoo and a list of timed events for the day. It is well worth earmarking some of the Meet the Keeper events and one of the Feature Shows as these are the real highlights that make this zoo so uniquely special.

The 20-minute long Feature Shows are held in the shady Safari Canyon Open-Air Theater, which has tiered seats overlooking the stage area. If you have small children the best places to sit are on the very front row, or the very back row where they can stand on the seat. There are also close-ups on large screen TVs. The show includes a lot of talking and is very informative for both adults and school children 8+. However, on my visit many families with younger children left the show early as the presentation did not hold the attention of children under school age.

The two zookeeper animators keep up a humorous and educational repartee assisted by a further zookeeper who shows the various animals to the audience. Animals in the show include a large sloth, a python, a skunk and a barn owl which flies across the arena in a beautiful silent display. The highlight during my visit was the young ocelot which actually jumped onto the keeper from one of the stands to great applause.

The admission ticket includes a 15-20 minute cruise on Lake Victoria which gives everyone a good view of the various primates, lemurs and monkeys. They all live on small islands and have plenty of ropes and trees to climb. Best of all, the animals are safely contained without any need for walls and fences. The guide gives an informative commentary about each animal and indicates points of interest along the way.

Follow the meandering paths around the Zoo and you will find plenty of picnic areas, drink vending machines and restrooms. There are also several places where you can buy drinks, snacks, ice cream and shaved ice. I found the staff members were all exceptionally friendly and talkative, from those organizing the boat trips to others serving the shaved ice. They all wanted to ensure we were enjoying our day and generally made the whole visit a real pleasure.

Visitors of all ages will find the giraffe-feeding a fascinating experience to either watch or take part in. For an additional fee, visitors are given several leaves of romaine lettuce to hand feed to the giraffes. One or more of the giraffe herd will be hanging over the gate and they reach down, curl their black tongue around the green leaf and eat it. This is a great photo opportunity and even young children find it absolutely thrilling and memorable.

Another add-on attraction is riding a camel along a dusty trail around the Cypress Hammock area of the zoo. Even if you do not participate, it is fun to watch and photograph.

Other Meet the Keeper Shows around the zoo include a talk about fossas of Madagascar, a coyote exhibit, a snake handling show, hand-feeding the alligators, a tiger event and a talk and close-up look at honey badgers, including learning how they got their name.

Additional Info

If you buy your ticket online there is a $3 discount on adult tickets and $2 off child admissions. There are no refunds, so the best tickets to pre-purchase are gift certificates and you still get the online discount. These are valid for any day, up to 12 months from the date of purchase.

Admission
Adults $19.95
Children 3-12 $10.95
Admission includes all shows and the Primate Expedition Cruise.

Note the generous discounts for booking online in the Additional Info section.

Cost of Additional activities:
Hand-Feed the Giraffes $5
Ride a Camel $5

Opening Times
9 a.m. to 5 p.m. daily
Closed Thanksgiving and Christmas Day

Where to Eat around Naples Zoo
The zoo has Wynn's at the Zoo Café near the entrance with a range of sandwiches, salads, snacks and drinks. At the opposite end of the zoo near the giraffe enclosure is Wynn's Jungle Café where you can enjoy a meal overlooking Lake Victoria.

There are ample picnic areas and tables in the shade for those who have brought their own picnic.

Nearby Attractions
- Corkscrew Swamp Sanctuary
- Fort Myers Beach
- Koresham Historic State Park

Billie Swamp Safari

Che-hun-ta-mo! (Hello!) from the Seminole Indians at Billie Swamp Safari. Visitors to Fort Myers may want to spend a day in the Everglades, riding an airboat and seeing the amazing wildlife in this Natural Wonder of the World. Set on 2,200 acres of untamed Florida Everglades, this authentic eco-attraction is further away, but it is well worth the drive. Located within the Big Cypress Seminole Indian Reservation, it is the largest of the five Seminole reservations in the state. A visit to the attraction offers the chance to see a wide range of Florida wildlife, visit an authentic Seminole encampment and meet members of the Seminole tribe who live and work on the reservation. You can even stay overnight in one of the rustic Chickees lining the airboat trail, and who knows what you will see and hear!

A day at Billie Swamp Safari is far more than just another airboat ride. The attraction includes wildlife exhibits, a Swamp Buggy Eco-Tour, airboat tours through cypress domes, alligator feeding and excellent Snake and Critter Shows.

See Rangers handling all types of exotic wildlife and dine on alligator tail, frog legs or more orthodox fare in the Swamp Water Café.

Location
Located off I-75 between Fort Lauderdale and Naples.

30000 Gator Tail Trail
Clewiston
Tel: (800) 949-6101 or (863) 983-6101

www.seminoletribe.com/safari

GPS Coordinates: 26.431, -81.041

Directions
Take I-75 east to exit 49 then head north 19 miles to the park entrance.

Things to Do at Billie Swamp Safari
The drive to Billie Swamp Safari takes in plenty of farmland and flat prairie along the edge of the Everglades as Hwy 833 winds its way from I-75 northwards through the scenic Big Cypress National Preserve. It is an experience rarely found anywhere else and is a pleasant but slow drive, so allow plenty of time.

On arrival, park in the marked area and start to explore the animal exhibits, huts and wildlife that are located on the edge of the flowing river. Tickets and maps are available from the Welcome Center and offer single attractions or an all-inclusive pass which includes an airboat ride, a swamp buggy eco tour and the chance to attend all the live animal shows, making the pass particularly good value for money. Keep a check on the timetable as you enjoy the day so you don't miss the Critter Shows and the Alligator Feeding at the Gator Pit, which has stadium seating.

The airboat rides are on a first-come, first served basis from the dock and times are posted for the next airboat ride, so waiting is generally not necessary. The airboats hold 8-10 passengers and due to the incredibly noisy engine, riders are given earplugs before boarding. They certainly live up to the sign on the dock promising: "It is noisy and you will get wet!" The 20-minute ride is fast and exciting at times and there is plenty to see. However it is not a nature safari with a commentary as such – that comes with the Swamp Buggy Tour.

The airboat sets off along the trail through reeds and grasses and past the authentic native Chickee huts on the riverbanks. The water is fairly clear and shallow and the area is teeming with herons, limpkins, osprey, anhingas, vultures, fish and alligators swimming or basking on the banks.

The ride goes slowly through a forest of ancient moss-draped cypress trees with their protruding knees and it is very still and eerie. However it is a good opportunity to spot all sorts of wildlife in their native environment. The Seminole tribe has some unusual animals to see along the trip so don't be surprised to spot water buffalo, bison, wild boars, red African deer and even ostriches as you enjoy the ride through the wetlands. There is also the sign of the Six Tribes on the hillside and a statue of an Indian Head honoring Chief Billie to look out for on your airboat ride.

After all that excitement you may want to explore the animal exhibits which include a rare Florida panther. Alternatively, take a stroll along the boardwalk while waiting for the next ride on the swamp buggy. These big-wheel vehicles carry passengers high above the wet prairie edge of the Everglades, giving great views of Florida wildlife and an authentic Seminole encampment. The guide points out wildlife, offers a commentary and is extremely knowledgeable about the Florida Everglades, so feel free to ask questions.

Various shows take place at set times throughout the day and they are extremely informative and well-presented by one of the Park Rangers. The shows are suitable for all ages, from young children to adults as everyone will be fascinated by the procession of animals that the Ranger presents.

All the audience get a chance to see the animals close up, although in the case of the snakes and tarantula spiders you may not be too keen! However, as the Ranger talks about the animals and explains why even tarantulas are harmless unless challenged, everyone visibly relaxes and enjoys the 30-minute show.

I can certainly say the Critter Show was the highlight of the whole visit for me as it was so informative and well-presented. The Ranger handled a tarantula, a snapping turtle, a huge American turtle, an adorable white furry tamandua and a baby alligator. The Snake and Alligator Show is similarly informative and entertaining with a range of reptiles.

Additional Info

Throughout the year, Billie Swamp Safari hosts a number of special events. One of the most thrilling is the Big Cypress Shootout and Re-enactment of the Second Seminole War in late February. The 1830s re-enactment takes place in a grassy amphitheater and includes plenty of war-painted Indians on horseback ambushing soldiers.

There is real cannon fire and soldiers can be seen loading and firing their flintlock muskets. The event includes alligator wrestling, Seminole Stomp Dancing and the opportunity for visitors to try their skills at tomahawk throwing and primitive archery. There is also a Soldier Camp and plenty of Native American craft stalls.

In June, Billie Swamp Safari hosts a Swamp Kids Summer Fun Festival and in mid-July there is a Folk Fest Nature Celebration with folk music, vendors and art works.

Tips

You definitely need to arrive early at the Billie Swamp Safari in order to enjoy the full range of attractions in the all-inclusive ticket price, which is highly recommended.

The park is a long drive from anywhere, so it is worth setting off early and allowing a full day for your visit.

Wear a long sleeve shirt and hat to protect against the sun, and a liberal spraying of deet insect repellant as you are in the heart of the swamp.

Cost
Safari Day Package

Adults 13-61	$49.95
Seniors 62+	$45.95
Children 4-12	$35.95

Reduced admission (after 3.30pm) $30 all ages

Single Swamp Buggy or Airboat Tour

Adults 13-61	$25
Seniors 62+	$25
Children 4-12	$25

Overnight accommodation in native Chickees from $40
Check out the website for special offers and discount coupons

Opening Times
Daily 9 a.m. to 6 p.m.

Where to Eat at Billie Swamp Safari
There are plenty of shady places for enjoying a picnic if you want to bring your own food. However, the Swamp Water Café is better than most attraction restaurants.

The seating is in a spacious air-conditioned room with a separate section for local Native American residents, who can be seen dressed in their colorful traditional clothing.

The well-priced menu is extensive with a good choice of burgers, hot sandwiches, catfish, huge salads and more unusual fare. It is well worth taking the opportunity to sample some of the foods not found elsewhere such as frog's legs, bison burgers and gator tail nuggets. There are sampler platters if you really cannot decide!

Nearby Attractions
- Ah-Tah-Thi-Ki Museum
- Lake Okeechobee
- Naples Zoo at Caribbean Gardens

ACKNOWLEDGEMENTS

The author would like to thank Nancy Hamilton and Francesca Donlan of Lee County Visitor and Conference Bureau, and Gina Taylor of TrueTours for their kind assistance. Also thanks to my husband, Roger, for his invaluable contributions and support.

FOOTNOTE

Please note that all times and prices are correct at time of publication, but may be subject to future change. Visitors are advised to check the website or call ahead for current information.

OTHER TITLES

Look out for more books by Gillian Birch in this popular series:

- Days Out Around Orlando
- Days Out in Central Florida from 'The Villages'
- Favorite Days Out in Central Florida from 'The Villages' Residents
- 20 Best Florida Beaches and Coastal Cities

COMING SOON

- Days Out Around Naples
- Days Out in Orlando with Children
- Days Out Around Tampa and St Pete's
- 20 Best Historic Homes in Florida
- 20 Best Beautiful Gardens in Florida

These are all available in paperback from www.Amazon.com and your local bookstore. They are also available to download as ebooks.

Keep up with future publications at www.gillianbirch.com

ABOUT THE AUTHOR

Gillian Birch is a freelance travel writer and published author. As the wife of a Master Mariner, she has traveled extensively and lived in some exotic locations all over the world, including Europe, the Far East, and the Republic of Panama. Her love of writing led her to keep detailed journals which are a valuable source of eye-witness information for her many published magazine articles and destination reviews.

Describing herself as having "endless itchy feet and an insatiable wanderlust," she continues to explore Florida and further afield, writing about her experiences with wonderful clarity and attention to detail.

Gillian has a Diploma from the British College of Journalism and is proud to be a member of the International Travel Writers' Alliance and the Gulf Coast Writers' Association. Learn more about her writing as YourTravelGirl at www.gillianbirch.com